Take a Walk in the Forest

Bob Jordan

Take a Walk in the Forest
Bob Jordan

© 2013 Bob Jordan
All rights reserved

ISBN-13: 978-1-4903812-8-2

Text and photos by Bob Jordan
Design by Lighthouse24

Table of Contents

Introduction 1

Avoiding Timber Sale Shipwrecks 3

Pay as Cut or $/MBF 4
The Percentage Split or Captain Maximus Opportunity Plan 5
Creative Payment Plan 5
Lump Sum 5
Cash Scam 6
The Fox in the Henhouse Plan 8
In All of the Above Situations... 8
Recommendations 9
Asset Management 9
Avoid the Timber Tragedies 9

Working with the Garden 11

Weeds R Us 12
Beech Party 13
Ironwood 15
Hickory 17
Hemlock 17
"Frank" 18
Carrots 19
Thinning Out the Carrots 20
Wall Street Wizards 21
Crowning Glory 21
Last Gasp Syndrome 23
People and Trees 26
"Woodland Ghost" 28
"Gilboa" 31

35 Woodland Savvy
35 Cherry
38 Birch
40 Maple
42 "Pepperoni"
44 Deer Smorgasbord
47 "Getting Olt Ain't for Sissys at the 10 Point"
49 Planting: Let Your Mom Do It
50 Eco-Blarney

51 Photo Discoveries
52 Critters
62 Lead for Venison Exchange Booths
68 Trees
77 "Oil Patch Yeller Dawg"

83 From the Author
84 Credits

Take a walk in the woods with Treebob for some no fear forestry.

The purpose of this walk is not to intimidate the landowner, but to inspire him or her to manage the woodlot to its fullest potential and meet the landowner's goals. This is a "tech no fear" walk, so **no** Latin tree names will be used for maximus understandus, the **KISS** (keep it simple stupid) shall apply. You will discover that I like to use analogies & an occasional story to explain ideas or entertain. It makes the principals stick in your mind better. I have found through the years that it is better to have an analogy that sticks with you rather than techno jargon that is immediately flushed from the memory bank. If you want the class room effect, have someone read it to you in a monotone voice, take two no-doz pills and call me the second Tuesday of next week.

This walk is tailored to northeast hardwoods, my medium, but many of the principals are universal and can be applied elsewhere. The last section is a photo essay on some of the oddities we found in nature. Buckle up your boots and wade in. I hope you enjoy the walk, and find the hike both informative and entertaining.

Avoid Timber Sale Shipwrecks

A-hoy! The first section will be devoted to defusing some of the issues that generate fear in timber world by educating the landowner and making him or her more aware of the quick buck artists.

I am frequently asked, "What does a forestry consultant do?" People seem to have the impression that we sit in towers waiting to report forest fires or run around with goofy hats and badges looking at bugs.

A forestry consultant should not be affiliated with any timber user. The consultant should focus on working with individual landowners helping them to establish their goals and then realize those goals while at the same time avoiding the pitfalls and the pirates. It should be noted that not all timber people are of questionable character; in fact it is a very small minority of bad apples that taint the industry. The consultant can put the landowner in touch with the good guys.

The following instances are true; the names have been changed to protect the foolish. Captain Quick Buck is the unscrupulous timber pirate. Black Beard is the pirate that buys from Captain Quick Buck. Freddie Frugal is the unwary landowner. There are special guest appearances by Ensign Easy and Captain Courageous.

Some frugal folks clip coupons, dutifully send in the rebates, buy their gas at the local station on super saver Sunday, and worry about that $1/2\%$ interest at the bank. All of these things are perfectly fine thing to do, BUT...

These same frugal folk's brains somehow turn to mush when... AHOY Captain Quick Buck shows up with a bag of cash to buy their trees. I have yet to figure why Freddie Frugal sells his timber to Captain Quick Buck for $30,000 and the Captain turns around and sells the contract to Black Beard for $160,000. The pirates just sank the ship folks. The timber, if managed correctly, could have sent the kids to college, supplemented the retirement, and still been an attractive and usable entity for Freddy and his family. It could have out-produced the $160,000 figure, leaving a good investment vehicle for Freddie's heirs. Now the woodlot is in shambles, the asset liquidated for his lifetime (at a fraction of its value) and may have repercussions for the next generation also. The ship has been scuttled. Captain Quick Buck laughs all the way to the neighbors for the next victim. "Hey, your neighbor sold me his trees so why don't you?"

An outline of a few pitfalls:

Pay as Cut or $/MBF

The landowner is paid on how much is cut when it is cut, hence $ per 1000 board foot (MBF). The more that is cut, the more he should get, usually involving stipulated prices. The pay as cut program does not get capital gain treatment. Proceeds get lumped into ordinary income creating additional tax loss lumps for the landowner. The pay as cut program, in the eyes of the law, makes the landowner the employer in a logging operation hence he is responsible for his employees, workmen's compensation, liability and exposes himself to unnecessary risk. If someone is injured on the job, guess who is responsible? Not Captain Quick Buck.

The pay as cut method is also a recipe for high grading (when the Captain cuts the best and leaves the rest).

When Captain Quick is the one determining what is cut, why are we surprised when the best quality trees of the most valuable species are cut and the least valuable trees of the lowest quality are left? If you were buying apples by the pound, would you pick any bad ones if you did not have to? If the captain pays a good price per 1000 board foot, you can bet the best part of the tree will go and two thirds of the tree (lower value) will remain in the woods unpaid for. This practice results in a net loss for the landowner.

The Percentage Split or Captain Maximus Opportunity Plan

This is the 50%-50%, 60%-40%, 70%-30% split programs, where the landowner and buyer split the proceeds by percentage. There is even a 0% -100% plan that promotes Captain Quick to General... General Larceny to be exact. Again there is no capital gain treatment, the landowner is the employer and at risk. Foremost, who wants to sell their timber for 50% of what a mill determines it is worth after it arrives. This is a scary situation when Captain Quick knows where more than one mill is. The upstanding captain simply takes the timber to two different mills and pays Frugal Freddie his percentage from one mill receipt...anybody good at math? How about $1/2$ of a $1/2$ (maybe) split on the 50-50 plan. There is another twist to the percentage plan: the expenses (cutting, skidding, and trucking) are taken out before the split is made. Check your math on that plan. You pay for the work and then split the remainder.

Creative Payment Plan

This was a good one used years ago. The Captain puts a dollar down to bind the agreement and to make it legal. The agreement states he will pay some fantastic balance when he cuts the last tree. Guess what? The last tree never gets cut. So Freddie sells all his timber for a buck and it is legal.

Lump Sum

Lump sum sales get capital gain treatment and the landowner is not considered the employer. The buyer is cutting the trees he has purchased. Of course Freddie must understand and know what he is selling and what the future for the timber stand will be after the harvest.

This would be a good time to discuss diameter cuts. A diameter cut means the purchaser can cut anything he wants down to a certain size. If all trees that meet a certain diameter are cut, including the weed and poor quality trees, there is a small glimmer of hope for the woods. This sets the woods up for future diameter cuts as the trees will be close to the same size or even aged in the future. Diameter cuts often promote the high grading scenario again. Freddie would not go through his garden and pull out the tomato plants and leave the ragweed, but he will let Captain Quick cut the tomato plants (cherry, hard & soft maple, oak ash) and leave the ragweed (beech, hickory, hemlock) so long as he stays within the size limits — kinda (we will go into this later). This effectively removes the desirable seed source for future generations of "tomato plants." The Captain loves tomatoes!

There has been a relatively new twist to the diameter plan. The Captain promises not to cut anything under 44 inches. He, of course is referring to circumference at *ground level,* this equates to 14 inches in diameter. Think about the shape of a tree. **Trees bell out at ground level,** some species more than others. An oak tree that is 14 inches at ground level might only be 6 or 8 inches in diameter breast high. Remember Black Beard? He bought the trees down to 44 inches and actually was cutting smaller ones. Black Beard was questioned about this so he proceeded to go back and cut the stumps off lower or at an angle to meet the 44-inch rule. Not a good plan for Freddie.

Often these operators realize 200-300% profit at the landowner's expense and win the title of "timber Jockey". Avoid the timber jockey and be well represented by a consultant.

Cash Scam

Captain Quick will give you cash! Ever see $30,000 cash? This is a license to steal and now the Captain owns Freddie for a fraction of the value of the trees. He then sells the contract to Black

Avoid the timber jockey

Beard for $160,000 and tells him not to worry if he cuts some trees smaller than the contract size – because the Captain has waited until after the first of the year, he knows Freddie has filed his taxes and not claimed the cash. If Freddie Frugal complains about smaller trees being cut or no clean up, or even the trees next to his house being cut, the good Captain tells him to be quiet or he will turn him in for not reporting. The Captain owns poor Freddie.

We had a bid opening a number of years ago and Ensign Easy showed up at the landowner's house the day before the bid. He tried to sway the landowner to sell everything down to 14 inches, on the stump, for $10,000 cash, today only, one time offer, all bets are off if she waits for the bids! The landowner didn't bite. We got the landowner $47,500 on that select cut. Four years later, because of a medical emergency the landowner had to sell it fairly hard (but still not even down to 14 inches DBH, diameter breast high, not at ground level) and got $103,770. Sorry Ensign Easy.

Captain Courageous bought a piece of timber down to 14 inches on the stump. This captain then duped the landowner into giving him an additional 10 years on the contract for an extra $1,000. During the ensuing 9 years the good captain made a small select cut like Mr. Mush for brains should have. The marginal trees that would not have made the minimum diameter could now grow and would make the diameter limit. So this captain was able to cut many more trees 9-1/2 years later. Oh, by the way, did I happen to mention that this is when hard maple doubled in value? Guess what kind of trees they were.

The Fox in the Henhouse Plan

The company forester or self-designated forester offers his services for *FREE* or *HALF PRICE!* Keep in mind who is the person who signs his paycheck or does he deal with only one logger or mill... whose best interests are being served here? If the "bargain forester" suggests you have someone of his choosing cut the trees and ship them to a mill where a value can be determined and you are paid later, pin your ears back and run 180 degrees the other way as fast as you can before *you* earn the Captain Zero award. The cut-rate captains quite often purport to be harvesting for wildlife. I have yet to see the connection between cutting all the oak and cherry in the name of wildlife. There are many things that can be done to improve wildlife that do not involve removing the most valuable trees.

In All of the Above Situations...

...there is one common thread. The sale of timber evolves around what Captain Quick Cash and his crew's objectives are. This is the major flaw in the process. The landowner's objectives should be first and foremost. Always look for the motivation. The Captain and his crew are trying to buy as much timber as they can as cheap as they can. This is contrary to what any landowner's objectives should be, it is a win-lose plan.

A private forester should be motivated to listen to the landowner's needs and work with those objectives in hopes that he gets invited back for future sales made possible by his efforts. I am reminded of the old men sitting around the pot-bellied stove in a country store. The little boy comes in and one of the men always asks the little boy if he would rather have this great big nickel or this little bitty dime. The little boy chooses the great big nickel every time amongst clouds of laughter. Unable to stand it any longer the shop keeper runs into the little boy and explains that the little bitty dime is worth twice as much as the great big nickel to which the boy replies "I know, but if I picked the dime we would never play the game again."

This is not a game for captains; however it should be the game for landowners and their foresters. Grab the dime and the game is over. Settle for nickels and play the game over and over and over.

Recommendations

Our firm recommends the lump sum sale with the landowner's objectives being represented, and the return maximized through competitive bidding within these parameters. The motivation of the consultant is to do a good job, leave future cuts so he can get invited back for the landowner again, and again, and again. This is a win-win situation, the nickels add up for everybody.

Asset Management

Treat your timber like the long-term investment it is and it will treat you well. Would you buy a high interest certificate of deposit that matures in 10 years and cash it in a week later or plant that garden in May and harvest it in June? Don't cash in those "44 inch" / small trees (green tomatoes).

Avoid the Timber Tragedies

Look at your woods as a long term asset, treat it with respect and it will turn into something positive for you and your family's future.

A good consultant will offer: sound silviculture, manage for species composition, stand stratification, and future cutting rotations. Good marketing skills: leave some nice trees for future first impressions by reputable buyers. The infrastructure is established after the first cutting, boundary lines, skid trails, and landings have already been determined. To a consultant, having clients that know what to expect, is a treat.

The buyers need the raw material to supply their operation. We play the players. It can get interesting. People seem to think there is some kind of voodoo magic to bidding. We have had buyers bid: their odometer reading, license plate number, wife's birthday, repeating/sequential numbers, rifle calibers, phone number, and just plain personal lucky numbers. Marketing is an arena where people are involved, consequently anything can happen. Some buyers will use the bidding process to send a message to their competition with the net result benefiting the landowner.

A consultant with good marketing skills makes his commission many times over for the landowner. A well-established consultant brings respect within the industry into the landowner's equation. There are no surprises for the buyer, he knows what is expected because he has dealt with the forester before. A good consultant's experience and reputation, not how many clubs he or she belongs to, will do more for you. Build that future together with your forester. Get your ship in shape; don't be afraid to set sail with good help at the helm. There are plenty of reputable buyers/operators that will work with the forester and landowner. Make all the Captain Quick Bucks walk the plank and then set a course that avoids the pirates.

Working with the Garden

Think of your woods as if it was a big garden. You just cannot pick your woods every year like a garden. Most people would not plant a garden in June expecting to pick it in July but they quite often sell their trees before they are ripe. Remember Captain Quick? 44 inches = 14 inches diameter at ground level = 6" to 8" DBH (diameter breast high 4-1/2 ft). Let us examine dbh.

Very few trees are perfectly round, for that reason we diameter tape them. If you have a tree that tapes 14 inches dbh, that measurement includes the bark. Not many people want boards made of bark. Logs are scaled inside the bark at the small end of the log. Trees are conical in shape. So you do not have to go too far up a 14-inch, diameter outside the bark, tree before you have reached a minimum sawlog diameter of say 10 inches inside the bark. In effect, if you have a tall 14-inch dbh tree you will be throwing away all that potentially merchantable portion of the tree above that minimum inside the bark diameter. This is a tremendous loss. Selling such trees is like cashing in the highest interest certificate of deposit before it matures.

Let that desirable tree accrue enough girth to make use of that merchantable height potential and the volume grows exponentially. Often log buyers set the grades, hence value, by diameter minimums. You could have a clear, no knots, log 10 inches inside the bark on the small end and it will be priced at a lower grade than the same quality of log that meets the larger minimum size requirement. This constitutes a double whammy in the selling of the high interest certificate of deposit / small diameter scenario. The other side of the coin is that if one allows that tree to reach its full potential, that exponential growth in volume and increase in grade value can be yours. Don't pick the tomatoes before they are ripe.

One would hope that the gardener would not go through his garden and pull out all the tomato plants and leave the ragweed. As ridiculous as this appears, people do it all the time in their woods garden by allowing the purchaser who is motivated to buy the best and leave the rest. The classic is buying all the hard maple cherry etcetera and leaving the beech and hickory for the squirrels.

Back in the 70s I had a call from a man who needed some money to fix his over-the-road truck. I was familiar with the property from Easter excursions in my youth. I soon discovered that there were numerous fresh oak tops (the leaves were still on them). I should mention that **at this time oak was worth much more than maple.** I ran to his house, where he was working on the truck, and mentioned the fresh cut oak. He told me a nice man had graciously helped him get rid of those "nasty old nut trees" but had left the beautiful maples. He should have had a scarecrow for his garden.

Weeds R Us

There was a fine gentleman who called me years ago because he had this 130+ acres that he had owned for 38 years letting it amass great wealth for his retirement. He had bought the property from a long extinct lumber company. I had the honor of explaining to him that his retirement would have been much greater if he had weeded his garden at the beginning of the growing season, 38 years earlier. The previous owner had picked the tomatoes, left the ragweed. The big old hollow beech and hollow hemlock trees did not get up and walk off his property. They just got bigger and more worthless, and took up more of the garden. **There is no bad tree fairy that will come in and remove the ragweed trees** (beech, ironwood / hop hornbeam, hickory, hemlock).

Beech party

Beech can be the ragweed nightmare. A root-suckered overstoried tree can survive because it is feeding off the parent tree. Beech has always been a low value species. Loggers have historically perpetuated the notion that it would be nice to cut the valuable trees and leave the beech for the squirrels. If you find a hollow beech with a squirrel hole in it and there is a cherry tree within a $1/4$ mile, you will probably find the remnants of cherry seed at the base of the beech or inside it. Squirrels seem to find comfort in cherry seed. Deer, raccoons, bear, birds, and just about everything likes cherry. There are some other "people reasons" for the over abundance of beech. When this country was expanding and railroads were being built, oak was used for the railroad ties. Many people in the northeast sold all their oak, kept the hard maple (because you could always use them to make maple sugar) and left the beech to fire the evaporator to make the sugar or make beech barn beams.

Cherry seed inside hollow beech

A standard prescription for most woodlots in the northeast is to have a "beech party." This can become a lifetime struggle, as often when the beech is cut, root suckers take over the site and "beech brush" becomes the new buzzword. Beech is more death defying than Evil Knievel. You can cut it and it will stump sprout. You can girdle it and it still hangs on for years and always there are those root suckers.

Beech with its smooth grey bark tempts the carvers for recording historical events "1960 snow was ass deep"

Girdled dead beech

Stump sprouts gone wild

Ironwood

Ironwood or hop hornbeam is quite common in our area. Ironwood dominates the site beating the desired species out. The problem with the ironwood is the physiology of the tree gives it a short life span. It dominates the site preventing something good from happening and then quits before it attains any kind of size.

Ironwood / hop hornbeam

American Chestnut burr

We still find Chestnuts, but they usually don't last long after they start producing burrs

American Chestnut leaves

Hickory

Hickory has been historically low in value. I always quantify this, because if you have hickory cabinets in your kitchen, then you know it is not low value. Hickory is hard to dry. It warps, cups, bends, checks, and so consequently there is a lot of loss in the value added portion of handling from stump to kitchen. Hickory can be a fooler. Like beech it can look fine on the outside and be hollow on the inside. Commercially it is the bitternut hickory that mills deal with. The shagbark hickory loggers hate, as even the bark is hard, and dulls their saws. Shagbark has the sweet nut that deer and people find desirous, and if you haven't guessed it, the bitternut is not as tasty.

Shagbark hickory

Bitternut hickory

Hemlock

Hemlock has a couple of pluses in one's garden. If the landowner likes his wildlife, low hemlock affords thermal cover for the deer, a motel where deer can go on those sub-zero nights. We have come to recognize over the years that some of the better

Bob Jordan

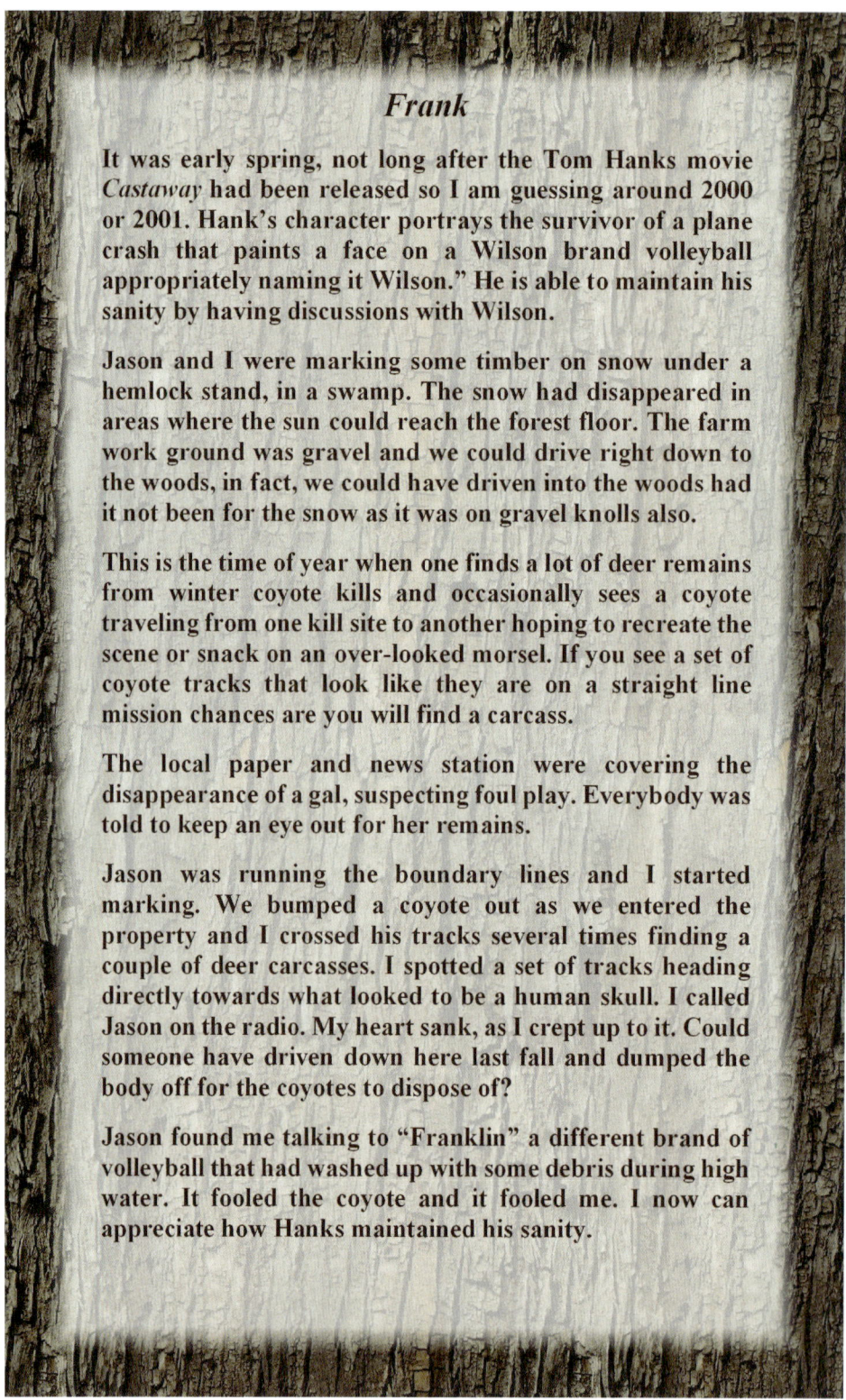

Frank

It was early spring, not long after the Tom Hanks movie *Castaway* had been released so I am guessing around 2000 or 2001. Hank's character portrays the survivor of a plane crash that paints a face on a Wilson brand volleyball appropriately naming it Wilson." He is able to maintain his sanity by having discussions with Wilson.

Jason and I were marking some timber on snow under a hemlock stand, in a swamp. The snow had disappeared in areas where the sun could reach the forest floor. The farm work ground was gravel and we could drive right down to the woods, in fact, we could have driven into the woods had it not been for the snow as it was on gravel knolls also.

This is the time of year when one finds a lot of deer remains from winter coyote kills and occasionally sees a coyote traveling from one kill site to another hoping to recreate the scene or snack on an over-looked morsel. If you see a set of coyote tracks that look like they are on a straight line mission chances are you will find a carcass.

The local paper and news station were covering the disappearance of a gal, suspecting foul play. Everybody was told to keep an eye out for her remains.

Jason was running the boundary lines and I started marking. We bumped a coyote out as we entered the property and I crossed his tracks several times finding a couple of deer carcasses. I spotted a set of tracks heading directly towards what looked to be a human skull. I called Jason on the radio. My heart sank, as I crept up to it. Could someone have driven down here last fall and dumped the body off for the coyotes to dispose of?

Jason found me talking to "Franklin" a different brand of volleyball that had washed up with some debris during high water. It fooled the coyote and it fooled me. I now can appreciate how Hanks maintained his sanity.

cherry grows in or around hemlock, which is a bit of a dilemma because cherry needs a lot of sunlight to regenerate. Hemlock effectively blocks the sun to the point that hemlock, a shade tolerant tree, has a hard time regenerating under itself. I am convinced that the needle cast amends the soil to cherry's liking.

Hemlock

Carrots

Woodlots, like gardens, only have a certain amount of growth potential. It is up to the gardener to determine how this potential is distributed. If the gardener planted 1000 carrots in a 3-foot long row, what could he expect at the end of the growing season? The results are some mini carrots that could possibly be used for an oriental salad or garnish.

Too many stems per acre in a woodlot has the same effect, the stand is at a stand still or is stagnate. The growth is crammed into too many carrots. Fruit growers quite often knock half the young fruit off their trees during the growing season thereby allocating the growth potential to the remaining crop doubling their size.

Spacing is not the only concern for utilizing the growth potential. One should not waste the growth potential on ragweeds but direct it towards the desirous trees for future cuts (grow bigger apples). Species composition is extremely important. If you had 10 thousand board feet of beech hickory and hemlock (ragweed), you conceivably could realize $500.00. If you had 10 thousand board feet of nice hard maple, cherry, oak (tomatoes/carrots) you could conceivably realize $10,000.00. What would you rather have in your garden? This is not a trick question. This is why it is important to pay attention to your garden!

Thinning Out the Carrots

This is where I get on the soapbox with my opinion. There are two basic theories... thinning from below and thinning from above. Thinning from below essentially removes the understory, leaving the dominant trees to get large and "beautiful." By using this method, the trees that would have been there to replace the "ain't that a beauty" trees are gone. Once the beautiful trees are cut it is time to start over. Hopefully they have seeded in for the next cut 80 plus years out.

My problem with this method is in the financial planning portion of forestry. I have yet to come up with a landowner or a forester that can survive too many 80-year rotations. I obviously would rather thin from above, removing the larger trees and encouraging all the trees to move up the scale enabling the gardener to have more harvests. If one can get a woodlot stratified where all the successional stages are present (seedlings, saplings, poles, intermediates, & crop trees), then when a crop tree is removed and the forest floor is day lighted, seedlings start, and all the stages can move upscale. This ideal situation allows for cutting rotations sooner than the 80-year program. Every time you have a cut you get the opportunity to make corrections (weed the garden) and get paid to have it done.

It is better to eat carrots all during the growing season instead of having a few big ones one time at the end of the season.

The growing season has to relate to the person's life cycle. You should not wait until you are 90 years old to have the one big harvest cut and expect to utilize the proceeds to pay for that trip of a lifetime. If you do, that trip is probably not going to include skydiving, alpine skiing and mountain biking.

Wall Street Wizards

A healthy, stratified woodlot can be a good investment strategy. We have had clients who want to tweak their woods now, plan for a cut in 8 to 10 years or when their kid hits college, cut again 10 years later when they retire and hopefully get another cutting during retirement and all the while leave a viable wood lot for the kids and grandkids. The beauty of growing this garden is in the value accrued annually is not punished by the taxman annually, so it can grow without annual income tax set backs. The wood lot can give one financial peace as an emergency fund, some place to turn if a tornado blows the roof off the house without going into debt. You could call this your hedge fund as it can be thought of as a hedge against disasters. I suppose this makes the person that subscribes to the one cut thinning from below method could be considered a hedgehog.

Crowning Glory

A good woodlot gardener should have a few bumps and bruises from falling down while walking in your woods. You have to keep looking up while you walk in a woodlot, as a lot of the story is in the crowns.

As you can see in the diagram on the next page, the dominant "D" has the best look at the sun and when harvested will afford the same to the co dominate "C" and when the co dominate attains dominate status the intermediate "I" can move up to co dominate status and so on. The concern is with the over topped individuals "O" as they are, in all probability, not going to make it to maturity and are wasting that growth potential.

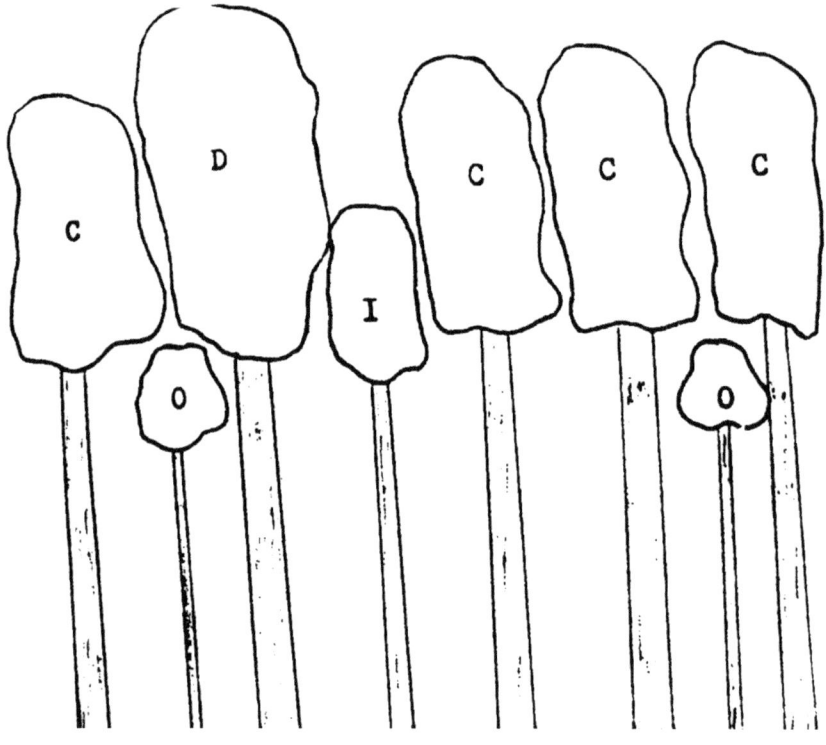

"D"- Dominant   "C"- Co-dominant   "I"- Intermediate   "O"- Over-topped

I had the privilege of attending a photo essay by a noted wildlife photographer. The man found a young fawn that was starving in a blizzard. He brought the fawn to his garage put an electric blanket over it, fed it alfalfa pellets and it still died. They dissected the deer, found the organs to be okay, but when they cracked open a bone they found the deer had used up its bone marrow.

The dead deer walking is comparable to the over-storied tree that can't get any sun. Often the over-storied tree will start sprouting and its top is dead. A tree in this condition, just like the starving deer, will not survive even if you released it by thinning around it. The whole time this tree hangs on it detracts from the surrounding crop trees sapping that site potential.

Last Gasp Syndrome

In nature living organisms are designed to perpetuate themselves or perish. When an organism becomes stressed or injured, it starts to cram for its final exam. Envision the lady who wants to win the blue ribbon for roses at the county fair, taking the crown away from her neighbor. She takes out a hammer, beats up her rose bush, gets the most lush or best flowers ever and wins. Have you ever nicked an apple tree with the lawn mower? This can have the same effect, producing a bumper crop of apples.

This is what is going on with the beech tree that is stressed by heart rot. The tree starts pushing out all those root suckers. Even if beech was desirous, the root suckers would trans-locate the heart rot from the parent tree. Again, these trees are wasting growth potential.

To successfully girdle a beech one must cut into the tree deep enough to cut the cambium (3/4 to an inch). The girdle must match or connect. Then drop down a few inches or so and girdle again. Next connect the girdles with opposing slashes being careful to hold the saw correctly to avoid any saw kickback (that could leave a nasty scar on ones face).

Girdled Beech demo

Now you know how to have a beech party without the sand.

Note: saw was not running as both hands should always be on a running saw

One should make the girdle where you are comfortable with the stump. If you leave four- foot stumps throughout your woods, it will be more difficult to maneuver machinery over them when you have a harvest cut.

A year after the girdle is complete and the tree greens up again, you will be calling your forester wondering what went wrong.

Have you ever gone to a nursery and bought a tree for say $25.00 and they say for an extra $10.00 they will guarantee it for a year? The tree should have enough nutrients stored up in its root system to sustain it for at least a year and maybe longer (save your money). Girdling as stated does not immediately kill the tree, but it is a very effective tool for the gardener.

Number one, you do not have to be Paul Bunyan with a monster saw to kill a large and potentially dangerous tree to cut, all you have to do is make sure you cut the cambium. Second, if it is a large tree as it dies out, it will come down in pieces with less damage to the residual stand. Just remember to tell your hunting buddies not to stand under it on opening day of deer season when there is a foot of wet snow and a 30 mph wind as they do come down eventually! Remember the old adage "Woodsman stay out of the woods on a windy day if you want to live to collect your pay."

The girdled tree dies out slowly and the rest of the trees take up the space slowly. The girdled tree offers some mutual support for the surrounding trees against wind throw until the trees that are being helped become more root firm.

Dead but still standing beech

We had a client who was inspired to girdle his aspen in favor of old apple trees to feed the deer. Aspen, like pin cherry, is pioneer species that kills very easily with a single girdle. True to form I get the call a month after meeting with him when trees have greened up. He proclaimed, "I thought you said it would take a long time for the trees to die? They are all dead." I had to see this. He had made sure the girdle was deep enough (three to four to six inches deep), we had a late, wet snow, and a windstorm, all his aspen was on the ground. We have the makings of a new game show called *Stump the Stumpy*.

Aspen, Quaking Aspen, "Quakies"

Pin Cherry

People and Trees

I marked a timber stand south of Buffalo in 1987. The farmer next door called to have me walk his woods with him to see what he should do. I met him at the farmhouse after morning chores and the first question I asked him was did he know where his boundary lines were. He responded that when he bought the property, his brother and him ran new fence wire around the wooded portion but we might have trouble finding it because the wire had grown way up high in the trees. Folks, this only happens in cartoons, usually involving Jack and the Beanstalk, but I kept my mouth shut. It was a good thing I did, because when we got to the woods sure enough the wire was way up the trees. Perplexed, I asked him just when he had bought his farm. He recalled buying his farm in January, 10 years ago adding his brother and him had a heck of a time stringing the wire. Lets see ... that would make it the blizzard of 1977 (snow must have been ass deep in '77 too). Chalk one up for not stumping the stumpy.

Trees grow by laying down annual growth rings around the circumference

Let's take a time out for an urban mythology lesson. Contrary to popular belief, that tree in the back yard is not the last valuable tree on the planet. The sawmill owners are not going to Fort Knox to borrow enough gold to buy it.

Woodland Ghost

Big Al was waiting for us in the driveway with his little Jack Russell terrier under his arm. He proudly put the little dog through a series of tricks culminating in putting him in our truck and instructing him to "guard the truck". He then instructed us to try to get into our truck. This cute little pouch immediately transformed into Cujo the wolf from hell. He opened the door and pointed to my arms and the little pooch jumped up into my arms licking my face, back to cute mode. I don't know who had more fun with this act the dog or Al.

We walked Al's woods with him and soon gained an appreciation for his love of critters and of his appreciation of his woodlot. We were instructed to tweak the woodlot to encourage it but stay away from his walnut tree as this was another subject of his affection.

Years later, Al was tragically killed in a truck accident and we were asked to sell some more timber for the estate. It was spring and we were working through the woodlot. It is always a ploy to try and maneuver the other fellow into the lesser trees and mark the better ones, kind of like a pick and roll basket ball move. This is what I thought Jay was trying to do when he called me on the radio "Dad come over here and help, a bird is attacking me!"

"Ya sure I am in some nice trees nice try."

"No, I am serious, it's a hawk and he flew into me and now he is sitting in a tree watching me."

This was all happening in the immediate area of Big Al's walnut tree. I couldn't see Jay as I approached the area so I yelled to him and he sheepishly peered around a tree and said, "Tell Al I was just measuring the walnut to see how much it had grown and was absolutely not going to mark it!"

continues >

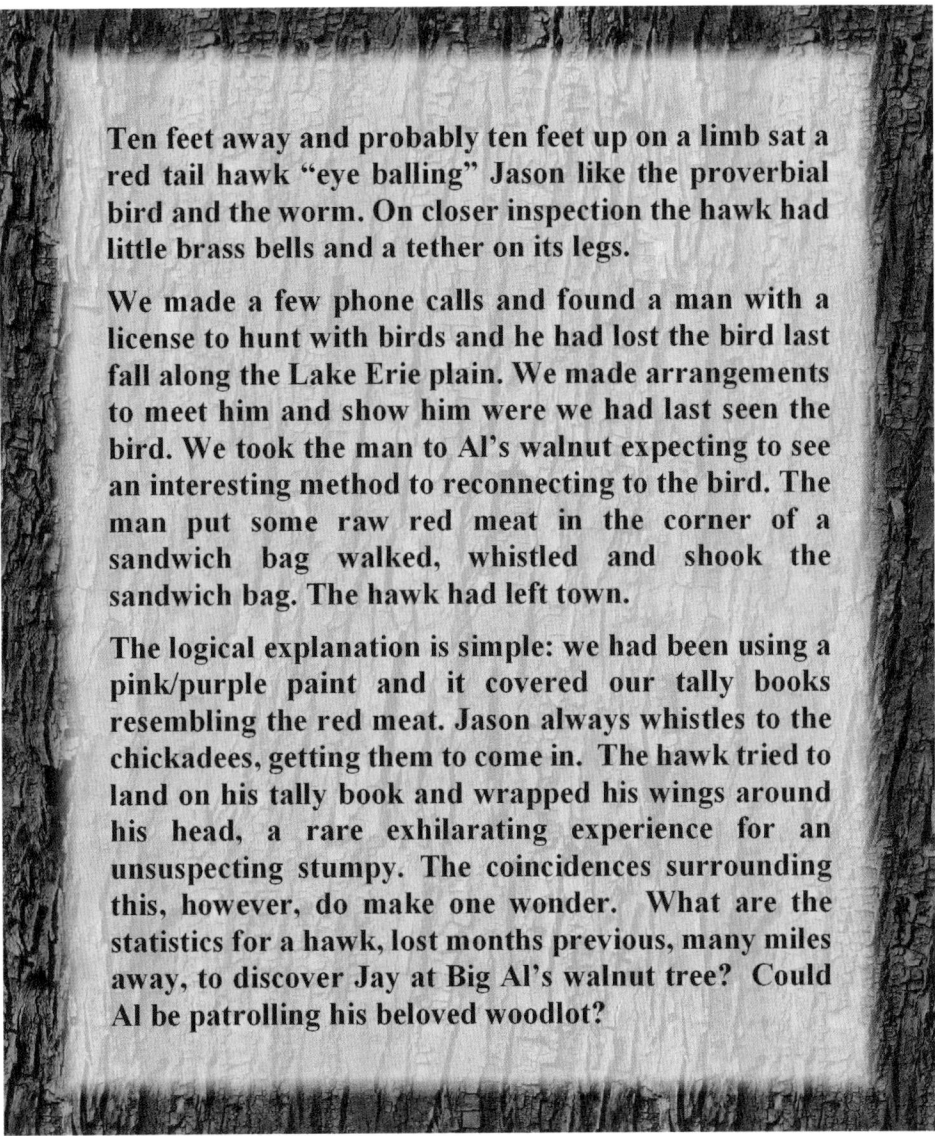

Ten feet away and probably ten feet up on a limb sat a red tail hawk "eye balling" Jason like the proverbial bird and the worm. On closer inspection the hawk had little brass bells and a tether on its legs.

We made a few phone calls and found a man with a license to hunt with birds and he had lost the bird last fall along the Lake Erie plain. We made arrangements to meet him and show him were we had last seen the bird. We took the man to Al's walnut expecting to see an interesting method to reconnecting to the bird. The man put some raw red meat in the corner of a sandwich bag walked, whistled and shook the sandwich bag. The hawk had left town.

The logical explanation is simple: we had been using a pink/purple paint and it covered our tally books resembling the red meat. Jason always whistles to the chickadees, getting them to come in. The hawk tried to land on his tally book and wrapped his wings around his head, a rare exhilarating experience for an unsuspecting stumpy. The coincidences surrounding this, however, do make one wonder. What are the statistics for a hawk, lost months previous, many miles away, to discover Jay at Big Al's walnut tree? Could Al be patrolling his beloved woodlot?

We get about one call a month for a walnut tree in someone's back yard. We had one not long ago we had to investigate because we were familiar with its location. The man's neighbors were complaining that his walnut was ruining their gardens. The tree shaded the back sections of four adjoining lots. Black walnut produces a growth inhibiting hormone that inhibits competition, lending some credibility to the wives tale that you cannot grow a garden under a walnut. The shade was also a factor. All the neighboring houses had squirrel damage where squirrels had chewed into the buildings for access to store the treasured nuts. The tree was completely surrounded by buildings, chain link and board fencing, phone lines, storage shed, and a dog house. A main power line support cable that had grown into the middle of the tree about sixteen feet high also lent incredible value. Needless to say I had to inform the owner of this treasure, that his prize possession was not an asset but a liability. The removal of the tree was not in the scope of work that would be covered by a logger's insurance and I would have to question the sanity of a tree surgeon who would tackle the job without the benefit of a helicopter. He assured me that the power company would cooperate as they did not want to deal with it. I should also mention that trees that are grown in the same proximity as people often acquire hardware. Walnut is especially famous for this as it has a nice cork board type bark making it attractive to nail up a clothesline, thermometer, bird house/feeder, a basketball hoop or a kids play house.

There are occasions when the back yard tree can be dealt with prior to it becoming a back yard. The young man gave us a call thinking he could sell the large white pines for enough money to help pay for the site work before he built his house. The trees were large and there was no doubt which way the prevailing wind blew. The tops of the pine trees were windswept towards the new home site. We strongly recommended the trees be removed prior to construction. The tree removal was more of a liability and not the asset he had hoped for. The decision was made to leave the trees and two years later the insurance company was called as his roof was smashed.

We had a lady insist we come and look at her trees. She emphatically repeated that she had "trees that have never been cut" We never got through to her that had they been cut, they would be logs. Standing on the second story in her kitchen we had to look out the back window at a hard maple and a cherry that had never been cut! The ground could not be seen from our vantage point but she assured me that the trees "went all the way" to the ground! In retrospect I guess she was right. She had trees (two), the trees had never been cut, and they went all the way to the ground. You are never too old to learn something. People can provide entertainment, even in stumpy world, I hope you find the following Gilboa story entertaining.

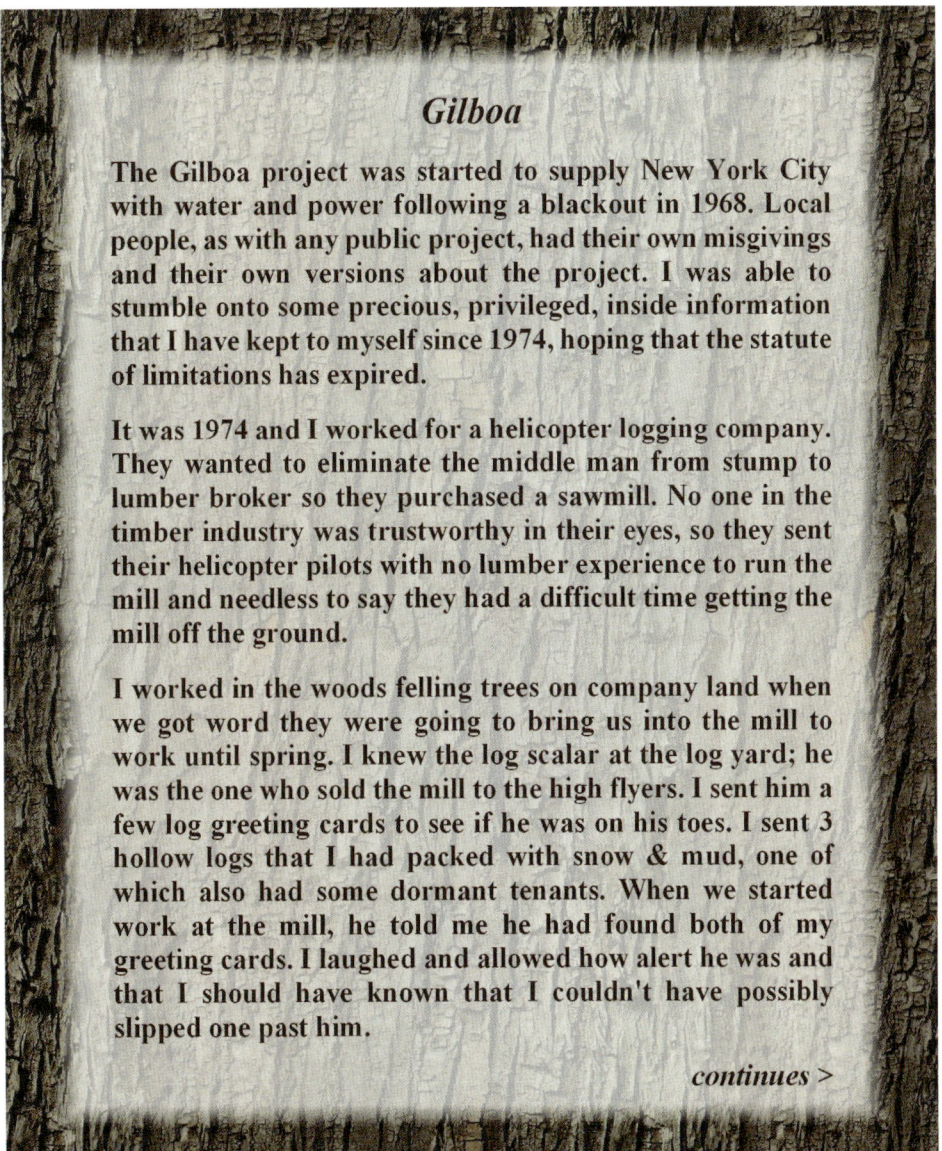

Gilboa

The Gilboa project was started to supply New York City with water and power following a blackout in 1968. Local people, as with any public project, had their own misgivings and their own versions about the project. I was able to stumble onto some precious, privileged, inside information that I have kept to myself since 1974, hoping that the statute of limitations has expired.

It was 1974 and I worked for a helicopter logging company. They wanted to eliminate the middle man from stump to lumber broker so they purchased a sawmill. No one in the timber industry was trustworthy in their eyes, so they sent their helicopter pilots with no lumber experience to run the mill and needless to say they had a difficult time getting the mill off the ground.

I worked in the woods felling trees on company land when we got word they were going to bring us into the mill to work until spring. I knew the log scalar at the log yard; he was the one who sold the mill to the high flyers. I sent him a few log greeting cards to see if he was on his toes. I sent 3 hollow logs that I had packed with snow & mud, one of which also had some dormant tenants. When we started work at the mill, he told me he had found both of my greeting cards. I laughed and allowed how alert he was and that I should have known that I couldn't have possibly slipped one past him.

continues >

Bob Jordan

Spring started to break and one of the mill hands, Arrogant Joe, had been bugging One Eyed Earl the log scalar/sawyer to show him how to run the head saw. This would surely garner him a raise if he could become a head sawyer. So it was arranged. During lunch break Earl would give Joe his first lesson. I was told to get a not so valuable log to put up for the wannabe sawyer to practice on. I knew the perfect one, been watching it for days. The inhabitants of greeting card log #3 were getting restless. The first pass into the log of higher learning sent everybody shuffling off to a better place to eat lunch, a place with-out any buzzing & stinging. Joe was not impressed.

The mill sent me with a logger Art Heart to buy his logs on the landing. Now rest assured you will not find a picture of this fella in Funk and Wagnall's under brains. He took me to his log landing where he had some white but small hard maple. The trees were small in diameter, so he had his crew (Mensa inter-national charter members) cut them all 8 foot, 4 inches (small diameter logs give you more scale when cut into short lengths). I scaled the logs while Art rode the crew hard about breaking all the four foot folding rulers. I told him that we always make a four foot stick with a groove at two foot. Art took a sapling cut it four foot two inches long and told them to mark out the logs with it. They could flip the stick end for end and make a mark on the log with a hand axe. The crew couldn't help but tell me about a couple of Art's exploits to help elevate their recently diminished social status. Art cut a tree on Franklin Mountain and it would not hit the ground. Determined, Art got his bulldozer and pushed on the tree until the power lines he hadn't seen came down with the tree.

Art the proud owner of the newest biggest chainsaw he could find, tried to start it in front of the crew to show it off. The saw would not start. In a fit of rage Art threw the saw into the middle of the landing, started the bulldozer and ran over the new saw. One of the Mensa gang then picked up the remains only to discover the saw never had any gas in it.

continues >

I finished the log tally and Art wanted to get paid. This was on a Friday afternoon. I told him the book keeper would be leaving soon so he had better plan on payment next week. Nothing doing, he said I got in the car with the tally and the speedometer seldom went below 100 MPH. Back at the mill, we did make it before the book keeper left. Arrogant Joe, the wannabe sawyer, was impressed once more. He was sure justice had been served, as tears of laughter streamed down his cheeks and a white knuckled, weak kneed stumpy bailed out of Art's car vowing to never ride with him again.

The following week I was sent to Art's log job to scale some more logs (I drove myself). The logs appeared to be short, they have to be 8 foot long with some trim. I measured the length and the logs were all miss cut, they all were shorter than 8 foot so they were worthless. The Mensa crew had nibbled off the end of the marking stick with the hand axe as they marked out the logs. Shortly after, Art sold the job to the company and we got out of the mill and back into the woods to take over the Mensa job.

Have you ever had that uncanny feeling that someone is watching you, that little tingle on the back of your neck? Well I had that feeling as I was cutting the Mensa woods. I shut the saw off and spotted some movement behind a tree. I hollered over towards the movement and Dave Deliverance, a real wood tick came out to parley. I had just gained his confidence and was going to ask him to vacate before he got injured when he asked me at low breath, if I knew about the Gilboa project. I said I had heard about it, but knew very little about it. If the statute of limitations has not expired I must now have your solemn promise that you will keep this in strict confidence.

The wood tick was upset at all the expense the city of New York had gone to. They did not need to build the big pond for flood control. They should have never taken down the towers (meaning the old fire towers). They should have put up more of the towers and they wouldn't have had to do any flood control.

continues >

When I asked him how that theory worked he said, "Them towers shoots out radars and that chases away them big new planes. The planes dey is bigger than they used to be. The old planes had propellers and they didn't hurt a thing, kinda mixed up the clouds without hurtin' anything. Them new ones suck up all the clouds. Ever see 'em suckin up all them white clouds? They drag them white clouds behind and when they get to the corner of the sky, the clouds get all bunched up and that creates a cloud burst. The cloud burst in turn creates a flood. So, they wouldn't need any flood control if they just would have got more towers to shoot out radars that chase away the big cloud suckin planes."

Now you know the real story about the Gilboa project, but remember your oath of secrecy.

Woodland Savvy

The last gasp syndrome does have a positive side. If a cherry tree is injured or is struck by lightning – as it often is – and is still hanging on, keep it.

Cherry

This tree, like the blue ribbon rose or the damaged apple tree, will throw fruit like it is cramming for its finals. The seed is genetically fine and every critter likes cherry. If you are an archery hunter and the cherry seed is hitting the ground, you will notice the deer scat is loose. There is a connection here. Raccoons, bears, coyotes, squirrels, and birds all love the seed so it gets disseminated.

Lightning strike cherry (at distance and close-up). Lightning loves cherry – the tree is full of moisture that turns to steam when struck and we get cherry toothpicks.

I always get the question from loggers, "Why didn't you mark that cherry I know it is going bad, can't you tell?" I would rather have a bad cherry than a good beech. (See the carrot section $500 vs. $10,000.) This is a case where the stressed tree can help as a good seed source of the desired species.

Beaver-chewed cherry, deer browsed sprouts, still alive

I often get called by someone who poses the question, "I got a cherry tree, what's it worth?"

My standard answer is: "How much is a 1967 Mustang worth?" To this I add, "Has it been fully restored in showroom condition, or has it been out back of the barn where it caught fire after the engine and transmission were removed and then used for target practice?"

There is more to the determining value than identifying the species, just as with the Mustang. One tree seldom brings buyers on the run. This is like going to the store for one egg. People would prefer a dozen eggs if they are making the trip. So quality and the volume being sold will influence value. Access is also important. You could have the finest timber in the world and if you cannot get it out the value should be obvious. Species composition, are you trying to sell tomatoes or weeds? Average size matters, mature carrots are better.

Cherry (note hemlock)

Landowner's grasp of what to expect and how he relates to the buyer or his logging crew can influence value. I know a few buyers who will make it a point to ask directions or somehow meet the landowner before submitting a bid to see if he will be reasonable to deal with.

The local municipalities can influence value. There are a growing number of municipalities that have reduced resident's timber value because of zoning, local ordinances, restrictions, or permits. There are townships that many buyers will avoid completely or reduce their bid substantially to compensate for anticipated problems. That is an expense ultimately paid unknowingly by the landowner.

Often one will find cherry in conjunction with locust. Cherry is somewhat site demanding and loves the fact that locust is a legume so it fixes nitrogen in the soil. Locust will help refurbish the soil but is not a valuable timber producer. It is rot resistant and thus is used for fence posts. Turkeys like the seed also. Locust can be hard to handle (see photo).

Locust thorn

Birch

Yellow birch is a favorite browse for deer. Chew a yellow birch bud you will find the oil of wintergreen flavor appealing yourself.

The problem with birch is its efficient reproductive efforts. Often when trying to regenerate cherry, birch will carry the day. Birch will hold its seeds until conditions are right, usually after a thaw-freeze cycle. The snow thaws then freezes making a skating surface for the little crowfoot shaped seed to blow for miles (see photo).

Birch Seed

Birch often seeds in on top of a hemlock or pine stump, starts to grow and the stump rots away leaving a birch on legs.

Yellow birch

Yelllow birch seedlings on hemlock stumps

Older yellow birch after hemlock stump rots away — "Old Yeller"

Maple

I am often asked, "How do you tell the difference between hard and soft maple?" The hard maple has a rough bark (see photo) but the soft maple can also have a rough or smooth bark, or both (see photo). The soft maple bark, as it fractures will often display a rosette pattern (see photo). Soft maple bark is softer / breaks easier than hard maple bark that is harder.

Hard Maple   **Soft Maple**

Have you noticed we are paying attention to bark? A good share of the year when we are a-field, there are no leaves – so bark is the only game in town, plus mature trees may have leaves to high to see. Bark also gives us an indication of tree vigor.

I have many clients who are farmers. I would need their help if I owned cows as the only way I would know if a cow was sick would be if it was laying on its side, its eyes were rolled back and its tongue was hanging out. But a tree is a different story. I had a client once who announced the only tree he knew how to tell by its bark was dogwood; I think he was barking up the wrong tree. Frequently a farmer will ask, "Tapping doesn't hurt the tree does it?"

To this, I always reply that if I drilled holes in his cows would it help them? Most of them get the message.

Don't get me wrong many farm families supplement the farm with a sugar bush. Just don't expect top dollar for those trees when they are sold for timber and understand that it does put stress on the tree and affords a vent for pathogens and stain.

"Tubing is ok because the spiles are plastic right?" It still makes a hole and we find that people are inclined to make sure they have enough incline when they use tubing, so they will tap higher up the tree devaluing more of the most valuable part of the tree. If a spile is left in a tree, then plastic is better than steel, but please don't support the plastic lines with nails. The metal left in trees becomes shrapnel when it goes through the sawmill. If the hardware damages the saw it can be quite costly and the down time is not cost effective.

Tapped maple after butt cut off

We have a couple of critter problems with hard maple. Often the logger gets wrongly accused of skinning up maple roots when the real culprit is a porcupine or squirrel. The term porky's revenge comes to mind, particularly if you have a dog, A few less porcupines would not bring a tear to my eye. If you have a lot of porks in your woodlot, they are easy to locate in March or April. This is the time of year when they nip hemlock branches and it is very noticeable on snow.

We also have a cute little sapsucker that will girdle the top of a maple. He will make a junket around the woods hammering on the maple to stake out his territory and show off for a mate. The sweet sap attracts bugs for him in his absence. The girdled top dies and makes a convenient nesting cavity later on. Not my favorite bird.

Pork litter and scat

Maple top on the forest floor (note the bird peck)

Pepperoni

The deep red golden retriever pup made his debut by jumping into his water dish. His first act upon arriving at his new home was splashing all the water out of his dish. Months later "Splash" as he was dubbed for obvious reasons, loaded himself over the tailgate, into the back of the pickup and assumed the coveted "shotgun" position behind the passenger side. This was a coveted position from the previous deep red golden named "Shotgun Red."

Splash always made working in the woods interesting. We were working near a local gas n go so I didn't sack a lunch. Lunchtime I grabbed a piece of pizza jerky off the revolving warming rack and spotted a little chub of pepperoni next to the checkout. Back to the woods the pleading eyes knew the chub was for him and he got it one half at a time. It was either the timing, the dog had an affinity for burning off extra energy, or it was the pepperoni but the pup started doing speed laps around in circles and the term "pepperoni overdrive" was coined. The second chub was more like a NFL handoff between laps. I have seen dogs, calves, cats, in fact, lots of animals exhibit this behavior. I want to believe the instant rush of the pepperoni kicked the dog into overdrive, but I could be wrong.

We have watched a pair of fawns one of them is vigilant, stoic, mimicking the mom and barely blinks and the other fawn was in pepperoni overdrive more often than not. These were very definite behavioral identifiers. Pepperoni obviously became the nickname for the one fawn. This year he sported a forked rack and again his dog "donuts" and spinouts gave him away.

My wife has an aunt & uncle that spent many years in Texas before returning home where they grew up. The first deer season after their return Uncle Harry asked if we knew where he can get a "waller" not being familiar with the Texas term I had to ask. He said, "You know, a deer big enough that you would want to have it mounted on the wall . . . a waller." From then on when one of us figures out where a waller might be residing, the waller is as dubbed "Wally" and of course his residence becomes "Wally World."

Stay with me, this will all tie together eventually . . . . .

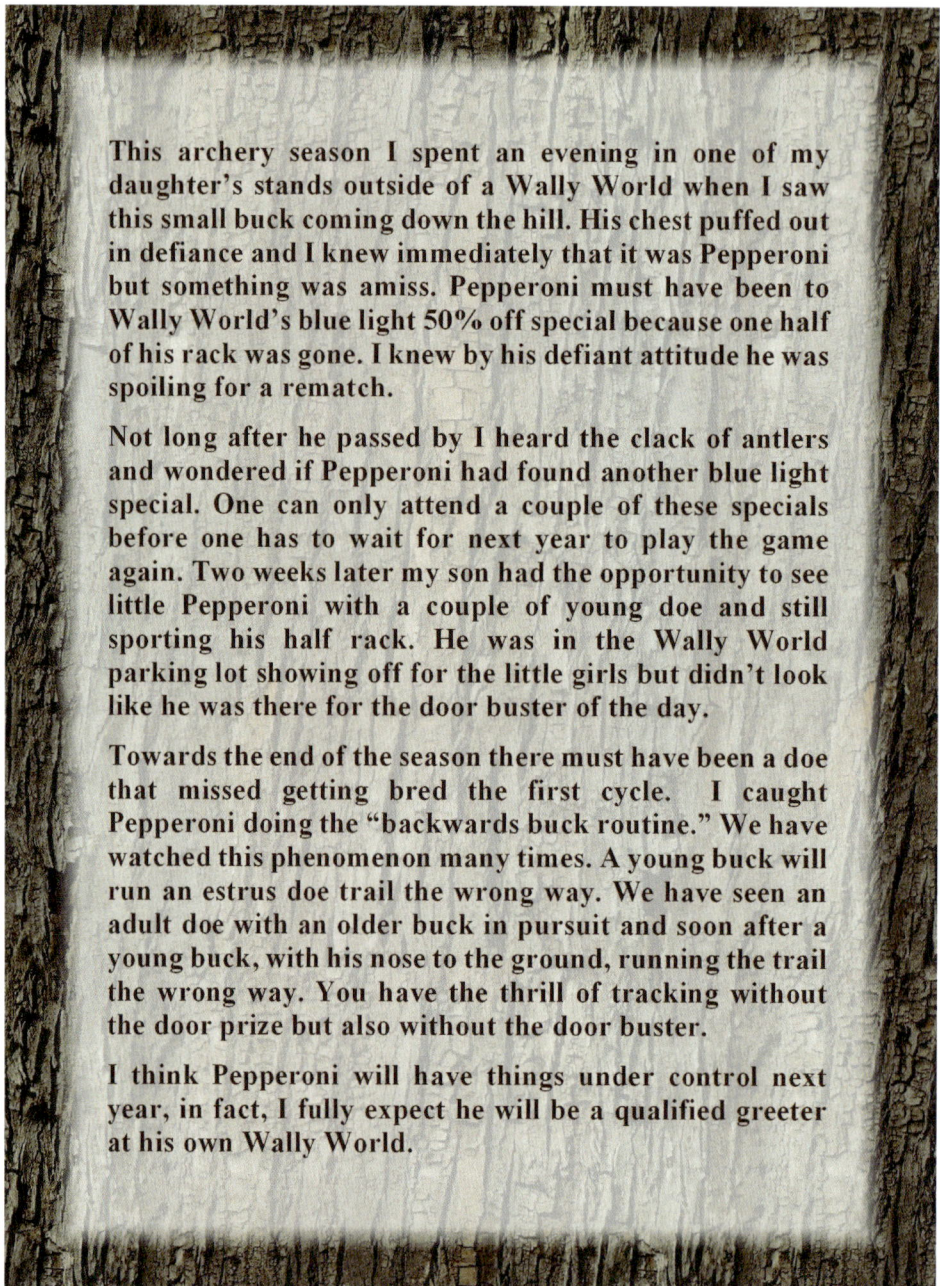

This archery season I spent an evening in one of my daughter's stands outside of a Wally World when I saw this small buck coming down the hill. His chest puffed out in defiance and I knew immediately that it was Pepperoni but something was amiss. Pepperoni must have been to Wally World's blue light 50% off special because one half of his rack was gone. I knew by his defiant attitude he was spoiling for a rematch.

Not long after he passed by I heard the clack of antlers and wondered if Pepperoni had found another blue light special. One can only attend a couple of these specials before one has to wait for next year to play the game again. Two weeks later my son had the opportunity to see little Pepperoni with a couple of young doe and still sporting his half rack. He was in the Wally World parking lot showing off for the little girls but didn't look like he was there for the door buster of the day.

Towards the end of the season there must have been a doe that missed getting bred the first cycle. I caught Pepperoni doing the "backwards buck routine." We have watched this phenomenon many times. A young buck will run an estrus doe trail the wrong way. We have seen an adult doe with an older buck in pursuit and soon after a young buck, with his nose to the ground, running the trail the wrong way. You have the thrill of tracking without the door prize but also without the door buster.

I think Pepperoni will have things under control next year, in fact, I fully expect he will be a qualified greeter at his own Wally World.

Deer Smorgasbord

I guess this would be the appropriate time to get on my soapbox again. I always make it a point to impress upon a landowner that he need not "clean up" the woods after a harvest cut. Nature grows the forest; man tries to make a park out of it. Too often people want to get the tree tops out of their woods and make it park-like. You will be doing yourself a grave disservice to get rid of the tops as they serve to protect the desirable regeneration from the deer.

Deer have expensive tastes. They like tomatoes (the cherry, maple, oak, ash) and dislike the ragweed (beech, hickory Hemlock). For this reason, the tops work as a mini deer exclosures. Deer are masters of energy conservation. They will eat what is easiest to get to. If they have to work through a tree top to get a few seedlings they will probably pass. The idea is to get the desirable species (tomatoes) above the browse line so they have a chance at maturity.

Most woodlots we visit exhibit what we like to refer to as weed wacker height cherry/maple/tomatoes. One will see the tomatoes browsed back to 6-8 inches about the same height you would expect to see if you ran a weed wacker through the woods while there was a snow pack on. Adjacent to the weed wacker tomatoes you will see beech/hickory/hemlock/ ragweeds that are well established and above the browse line. Deer are often the culprits when trying to get the garden in ship shape.

It may sound simplistic, but all the large trees started out as a seedling, root sucker or sprout. This makes paying attention to the regeneration extremely important for the future of the stand.

Weed wacker height
hard maple regen

Oak egg hatching for Easter
(wished it was protected by a tree top)

Tree tops also afford great nesting cover for turkeys/grouse. When a landowner has a harvest cut they should view it as a rebirth of the forest community not the destruction of an old friend. It is sad to walk into an over mature park-like forest and try to explain to a landowner why his dad used to see deer (trees were cut prior to him buying it 40 years ago) and now he sits there for 2 weeks of the season and is lucky to see two doe. The woodlot is stagnate, the canopy is closed, no sunlight can reach the forest floor and therefore nothing can regenerate or grow – hence no cover and no browse. If having deer on the property is an objective, I have never seen a deer that could browse a 40-foot tree. A chainsaw is a deer's best friend.

Remember the quakie girdling storey? Two years after the aspen holocaust, the landowner caught a thirteen point sneaking out of his "buck nest" and it is now on the wall. There are commercial properties in Pennsylvania where they will go to the expense of fencing the deer out until the regeneration gets above the browse line (they are trying to regenerate cherry). This is not a financial option, nor is it desirable for most landowners that own their property for the purpose of seeing deer. This does not mean that, in order to have deer one must "clean up the tops." Deer love the seclusion factor.

While on the deer subject I would like to dispel the myth that not shooting a doe makes for more deer, healthy deer and more bucks. We walked a woodlot with a hunting club and noticed the signs of severe over-browsing. We returned to the club house where a perfect chronology was displayed on the walls around the outside perimeter of the main room (the learning curve). The members named the 10 point club after one of the member's father's deer taken many years ago. They decided not to shoot any doe at that time and had arranged the successive deer racks in chronological order around the room complete with the dates. The racks got smaller year after year. The carrying capacity of the woods was exceeded and the whole herd suffered. The good thing was they started to harvest some doe and the herd health returned and the racks were getting better.

Getting Olt Ain't for Sissys at the 10 Point

I went to an outdoor show and noticed a small compound bow on display. I asked the vendor if it was a youth bow. The vendor replied it was quite the opposite "pull it back, 85% let-off, light weight, short axle to axle you could even sit flat on the floor and shoot it." My shoulder had ached for some time and I could not seem to shake it. I thought I would have to eventually forgo archery. The vendor said he would hold the show special price and I went to his shop the following week.

Wild Cowboy Bill from St Pete, MO showed up and sympathized with my aches. He is 20 plus years my senior. I wasn't sure if a bone bender (chiropractor) was in order. Figured bone benders were like voodoo and were only really good at getting rid of that weight on your back right hip where one keeps pictures of kids, driver's license, and such. In later years, one made a believer out of me when he put my back in place. That's when Cowboy Bill hit me with "gittin olt ain't fer sissys." We laughed, but there was something deeper and more ominous in his message.

The shoulder seemed better and life went on. A close friend was diagnosed with cancer and was given a year to live, a prognosis he dutifully completed. I spent as much time as I could with him. My aches and pains diminished completely.

My father had a close friend, a real spark plug, always on the go until he had a disabling stroke that landed him in a nursing home. My Dad would visit him and I would hear if his friend was having a bad day, a good day or a mad day. After reporting on a particularly bad day my father announced he just wanted to go fast, no nursing home. I told him to "watch what you wish for" and we laughed. A few months later he got his wish.

continues >

The old shack always had a damp and kerosene smell even though it had been upgraded with propane lanterns. The only way to cure the smell was with a good hot wood fire in the three legged stove, some seasoned hard maple usually did the trick. Clyde had found a nearly new four legged stove at a yard sale. He brought it to the deer camp and the first thing he did was to smash one leg off, throw it out into the brush and put bricks under that side. When asked about the wisdom of his actions, he replied, "There who wants to steal a three legged stove?" (a microcosm of our society's evolution).

The duties of opening up the deer camp are toilsome. The pre-season work detail struggles with it every year. One has to clean up the squirrel plunder from the surrounding nasty nut trees. Dust off the 10 point rack that gave the camp its name. The squirrel plunder and dusting being completed, it was time for the serious work, split some kindling, get a good fire going, tote the ice and beer and get the cards played.

The sun had set; the room had a blue haze from the three legged stove plume backlit by the sizzling propane lanterns. All the past trials and tribulations, especially the missed opportunities, (humorous harassment) had been rehearsed. It was Clyde's turn to deal. Clyde had nodded off. Bill gave him a poke… Clyde had played his last hand. Pete and Bill were jealous. Clyde had checked out at the top of his game. He was at the deer camp surrounded by memories, friends and doing what he loved best. When somebody asked Pete about Clyde's demise he replied, "Ya, ain't it great!"

Only when you can gleefully celebrate a friend like Clyde passing can you fully understand Cowboy Bill's adage "Gittin olt ain't fer sissys."

Planting: Let Your Mom Do It

Often we are asked, "Shouldn't I plant trees after a harvest cut?" This is more relevant in areas where softwoods are the only game in town. Some places in the south plant softwoods like corn. In the northeast, hardwoods are the best game in town.

Planting hardwoods is a lot trickier than stomping in a pine seedling. Expect a high mortality rate in planting hardwoods and therefore plant the biggest trees you can afford (again to try to get them above the deer browse). You should plant trees as big as you can or stay home. If you elect to plant hardwoods or softwoods I would avoid the "cheap" program small trees. I would much rather plant 20 big trees and have 18 survive than plant 50 small trees and have 20 survive.

Be mindful of where the seed source for your trees came from. This is why it is better to deal with the hand you have been dealt. Mother Nature is providing you a seed source that has been evolving on your property since the last ice age. Do you think you can outdo Ma Nature by planting trees from a seed source from another geographical location? Regenerate a woods – let your mother do it. Once mother provides it, it is up to you to work with it.

I am reminded of the story of the preacher walking down a country road and happens upon a beautiful farm, everything is manicured and groomed up to snuff. The preacher tells the farmer "God has blessed you with this bountiful farm." The farmer wiping the sweat from his brow says, "Yup, but you should have seen it when he had it all to himself." Woodlots do not just evolve into the landowner's wishes. There is no good tree fairy that will bring good trees to your woods just as there is no bad tree fairy that will make the bad ones disappear.

Urban myth moment: "Let's plant the cute little pine trees for seclusion from the highway." The trees will grow. Try to envision what they will look like when they mature.

Many years ago a man planted some evergreens next to his garage and along the county highway. Years later the trees started to interfere with the power line directly above. The power company took the tops out to protect the lines and he still had seclusion. He didn't like the looks of the topped off trees. The man could also now see that as the wind blew, the limbs had been scratching the siding on his garage. The once small cute trees were removed and the siding was replaced. Fast forwarding to a new owner of the property I see he has some new cute spruce trees along the garage and beside the county highway directly under the power lines. History repeats itself.

Eco-Blarney

It is soap box time again. *What will it be, paper or plastic?* The last time I checked, plastic is made with hydrocarbons and paper is made from wood fiber. We can grow trees; we cannot grow oil or coal. This is eco-manipulation. The plastic takes up less space and is cheaper.

The motivation is always the key. "Let's tell John Q. Public he should use the plastic and save a tree" makes you all warm and fuzzy, doesn't it? How about people with an agenda telling J.Q. Public to use an electric (from a hydrocarbon fired generator) hand dryer instead of paper towels in a public rest room, and save the world. Somehow using wood chips for fuel is recognized as being green, but it is bad to use trees for paper or anything else ... eco-manipulation of a nation of sheeple (people who follow along without questioning, sheep tendencies).

How many people save their tomatoes past their prime? When the tomato is ripe you pick it and more tomatoes grow. When a tree is ripe you pick it or just like the tomatoes you get fewer of them and they get rotten. I propose a new eco slogan "grow a tree" instead of the usual version "save a tree" there is a beneficial difference. The traditional warmth and natural beauty of wood that can be grown and replaced should never be displaced by re-manufactured trash unless you have been eco-manipulated into thinking so. Recycling is okay and desirable, but the notion that it saves some majestic tree in a park somewhere defies logic.

Photo Discoveries

In the spring of '08 we were working on a property in South Valley, NY that adjoins state owned land. Jason sat down on a log to take a break and a grouse took off. We knew there had to be a nest near by. It was only a few feet from where he sat down. We were unable to return the next day but two days later we brought our 4-wheeler up the hill to a spot near the grouse nest. We slowly crept up to it hoping to get a picture with the cell phone (grouse sit tight) and since we knew where she was, this was going to be fun. When we got to the nest we found feathers everywhere and the eggs where punctured. This is unusual, as a skunk, possum or raccoon will ravage the eggs.

We went about our work, meeting back there at lunchtime only to hear whitetail fawn squalor. We thought it was the misfortune of a fawn to run into Wiley Coyote. The blatting persisted so we took off running and came upon a fisher that had the fawn by the throat. It was going to challenge us for the fawn, but saw that we had him outnumbered, so it ran. Now this critter is like a 20 pound weasel and weasels are killing machines. If a weasel gets into the henhouse it will kill all the chickens by slitting their throats. Now, I am sure of what happened to the grouse and why the eggs were not ravaged but punctured. What a time not to have a camera!

A few weeks later, we were working three to four miles away and we chased a juvenile fisher up a tree. I stood there with my trusty cell phone and took a picture of it . . . it looks like a tree. Nobody, including me, could see the fisher on the cell phone picture. I tell this story because after all these years of seeing interesting sights in the woods I finally got the message (Why not carry a small camera with you, dummy?!)

Adult fisher

This was, in part, responsible for the creation of this book. So I will subject you to some interesting photos taken recently. This is divided into three parts "Critters," "Lead for Venison Exchange Booths" and "Trees." Enjoy.

Critters

We met with two brothers at their hunting camp and one of the first things they told us was the neighbor had seen a mountain lion. Fifteen minutes into the walk I said look at the deer. They couldn't see it because it was up in the tree. We affectionately call this kitty litter.

Take a Walk in the Forest

An adult doe skeleton up in an apple tree

While suturing up a cut on an old Texas rancher, the doc struck up a conversation with him and eventually it got around to politics. "What do you think of our newly elected officials?"

The rancher replied, "They are post turtles."

Not being familiar with the term, the Doc had to ask what a post turtle was. The old rancher explained, "When you are driving down a country road and you come across a fence post with a turtle balanced on the top ... that is a post turtle."

Seeing the puzzled look on the Doc's face the rancher continued. "You know he didn't get up there by himself, he doesn't belong there, he doesn't know what to do while he is up there, and you just wonder what kind of idiot put him up there to begin with."

The next picture is of a real "post turtle" he is wedged in the crotch of an aspen limb about 20 feet off the ground. We suspect a local red tail hawk put him there, where he became turtle jerky. Possibly we have a one legged hawk in the neighborhood in now.

Post turtle?

We quite often see deer and when it is hot they seem to go out of their way to walk in mud or find water to cool off in. This photo is of a doe showing the spotted youngster how to cool of and escape the deer flies.

Doe and youngster cooling off

Take a Walk in the Forest

How do you like your eggs? Fishers like them poached.
The nest is under a tree-top left from a previous cutting.

This is a "woods chicken" we came across.
We think it may have been in a fight or had a rough night out, because he didn't
make any attempt to escape and spent the better part of the day recovering.

I met with a landowner friend that thought he should thin some of his trees out. We walked through and decided to mark some for thinning and to keep him warm in the winter. Wood warms you twice, once while cutting and again when burning. While we were walking and marking, this grouse followed us, in fact we got paint on him, picked him up, let him go, and he followed us back to the truck. He likes to chase the 4-wheeler. The golden retriever picks him up occasionally. He gets "ruffled" but comes back in a few minutes, when he regains his composure.

Take a Walk in the Forest

This is a coopers hawk that thinks we are too close to the nest.

Ever see a piebald deer? This one is getting old and gray. She did have a brown raccoon mask and a brown stocking. Now even those are gray making her look albino. She thinks she blends in like the rest of the clan. She does have the advantage when snow flies.

Turkey fight.
These jakes are so wrapped up around each other they didn't notice us.
Is this the source of the term necking?

Mr. Lovesick

Hen getting ready to nest, good area, protected by
fallen trees and tree tops beech party central

If I don't move you can't see me — Mom said so.

A skunk dug out a ground bees nest.
Good way to spice up a meal (organic hot sauce with a real bite)

(Left)
Swarm of bees on a cherry.
They are docile at this time

(Below)
Shed deer antler.
One has to develop an eye
to spot these. We have found
that a rainy overcast day
works the best.

Bear sleep center

Junkyard dog in the wilds

Lead For Venison Exchange Booths

Coming soon to a secluded location near you ...

We affectionately refer to this as the
"Ebenezer Scrooge Lead for Venison Exchange Booth."
Note the reminders of Christmas past.

The Stairway to Venison

Take a Walk in the Forest

(Right)
The hillbilly high rise
beech condo near
Clyde and Martha's Vineyard,
Stables and Dude Ranch

(Below)
2-story with wood heat,
real county livin'.
Wanna sublet the lower flat?
Upper story quite loud
during November, quiet
the rest of the year.

Executive suite condo situated right on the slopes

Dutch-door deer gitter.
This one gets the craftsmanship award. Construction started out
with Deer John plans (one holer) and morphed into a Danish version.

Take a Walk in the Forest

Sanford & Son high-rise, a.k.a. the Tilton Hilton with railroad tie accents

Failed lead for venison exchange.

Recycling award.
Grandpa made swing set from scrap gasline pipe ... Grand kids out grew the swing set ... Grandpa makes stable deer stand that can be moved with grandpa's tractor

The re-tired tree stand.

Take a Walk in the Forest

(Right)
Designed with buck fever basket cases in mind

(Below)
Free ambulance ride for hunter exchange booth. The "roughhouse" — some assembly necessary, a real fixer upper. Comes equipped with an express lane to the basement.

Bob Jordan

Trees

"Camera … Action … Cue the trees!"

This is a maple on legs.

Take a Walk in the Forest

(Above)
I have always heard of rock maple furniture and I finally found a rock maple. This one must be left over from Woodstock, it is definitely stoned. I can't tell if it's eating it or spitting it out.

(Right)
These are kissin cuzzins.
"Does my butt look big?"

Bob Jordan

(Above)
Trees
tandem rock surfing.

(Left)
Luv handles on the beech

Spring wood

The Gossip Tree
This is a living horizontal cherry
that almost makes a complete circle (a "gossip tree").

This is a Boone & Crocket atypical cherry, record book for sure

This hemlock is ready to kick the next dog that shows up

Take a Walk in the Forest

(Right)
"Help, I've fallen and I can't get up"

(Below)
Express lane for vertically-challenged squirrels --
"The Trunk Line"

Bob Jordan

(Left)
Making a break for it, no more scent-marking guard dogs!

Sneaking through the fence.

Left a nasty welt/tattoo

Take a Walk in the Forest

(Above)
Beech with a broken leg;
in-grown deer leg bone ???

(Right)
The stork tree
delivering seedlings

A new woodland flavor: Blueberry cherry. You can pick blueberries off this cherry tree. Suspect a squirrel or bird planted the bush.

One good turn deserves another: Organic wood turning.

Iron/wood? Remnants of oil patch ingenuity.

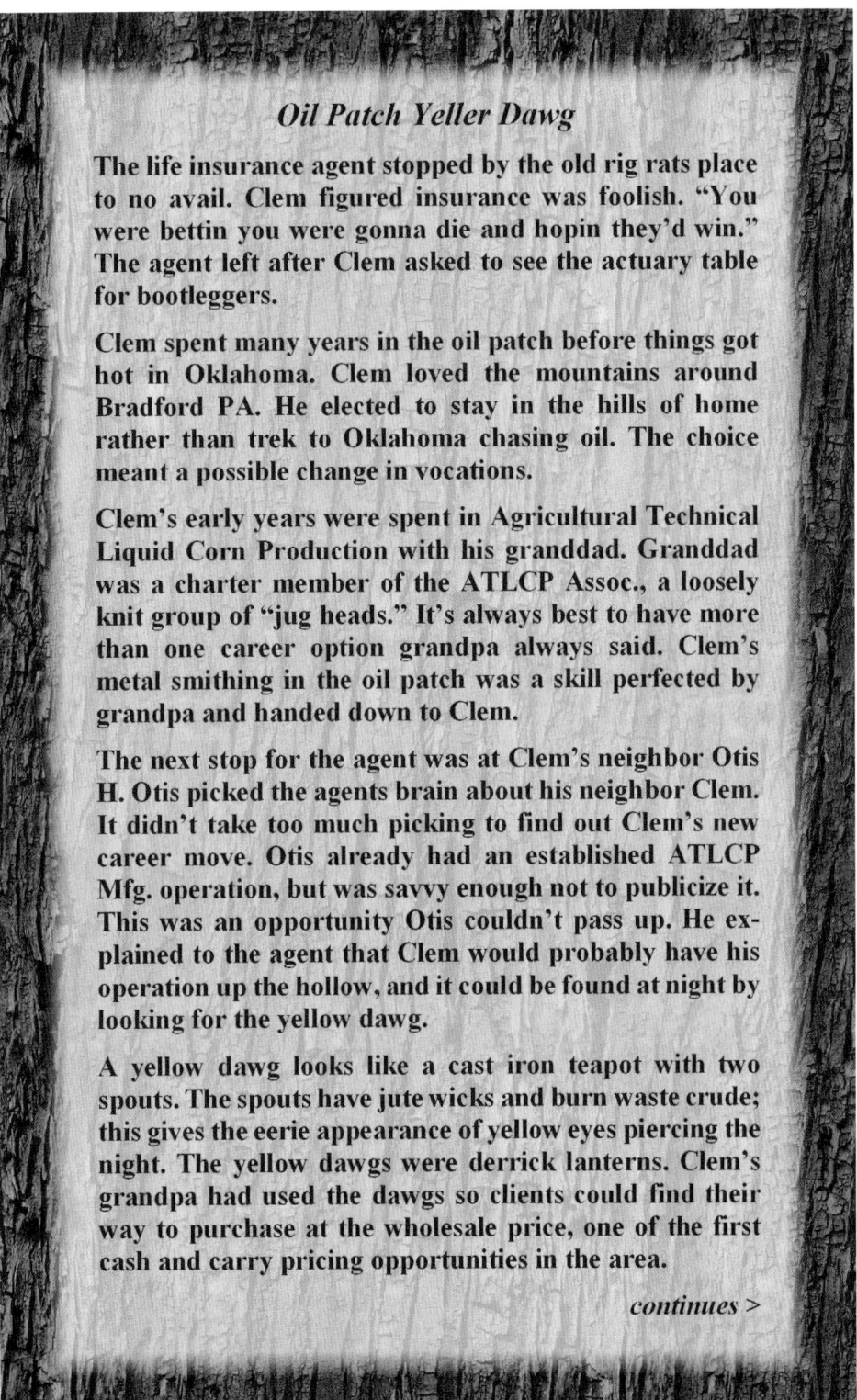

Oil Patch Yeller Dawg

The life insurance agent stopped by the old rig rats place to no avail. Clem figured insurance was foolish. "You were bettin you were gonna die and hopin they'd win." The agent left after Clem asked to see the actuary table for bootleggers.

Clem spent many years in the oil patch before things got hot in Oklahoma. Clem loved the mountains around Bradford PA. He elected to stay in the hills of home rather than trek to Oklahoma chasing oil. The choice meant a possible change in vocations.

Clem's early years were spent in Agricultural Technical Liquid Corn Production with his granddad. Granddad was a charter member of the ATLCP Assoc., a loosely knit group of "jug heads." It's always best to have more than one career option grandpa always said. Clem's metal smithing in the oil patch was a skill perfected by grandpa and handed down to Clem.

The next stop for the agent was at Clem's neighbor Otis H. Otis picked the agents brain about his neighbor Clem. It didn't take too much picking to find out Clem's new career move. Otis already had an established ATLCP Mfg. operation, but was savvy enough not to publicize it. This was an opportunity Otis couldn't pass up. He explained to the agent that Clem would probably have his operation up the hollow, and it could be found at night by looking for the yellow dawg.

A yellow dawg looks like a cast iron teapot with two spouts. The spouts have jute wicks and burn waste crude; this gives the eerie appearance of yellow eyes piercing the night. The yellow dawgs were derrick lanterns. Clem's grandpa had used the dawgs so clients could find their way to purchase at the wholesale price, one of the first cash and carry pricing opportunities in the area.

continues >

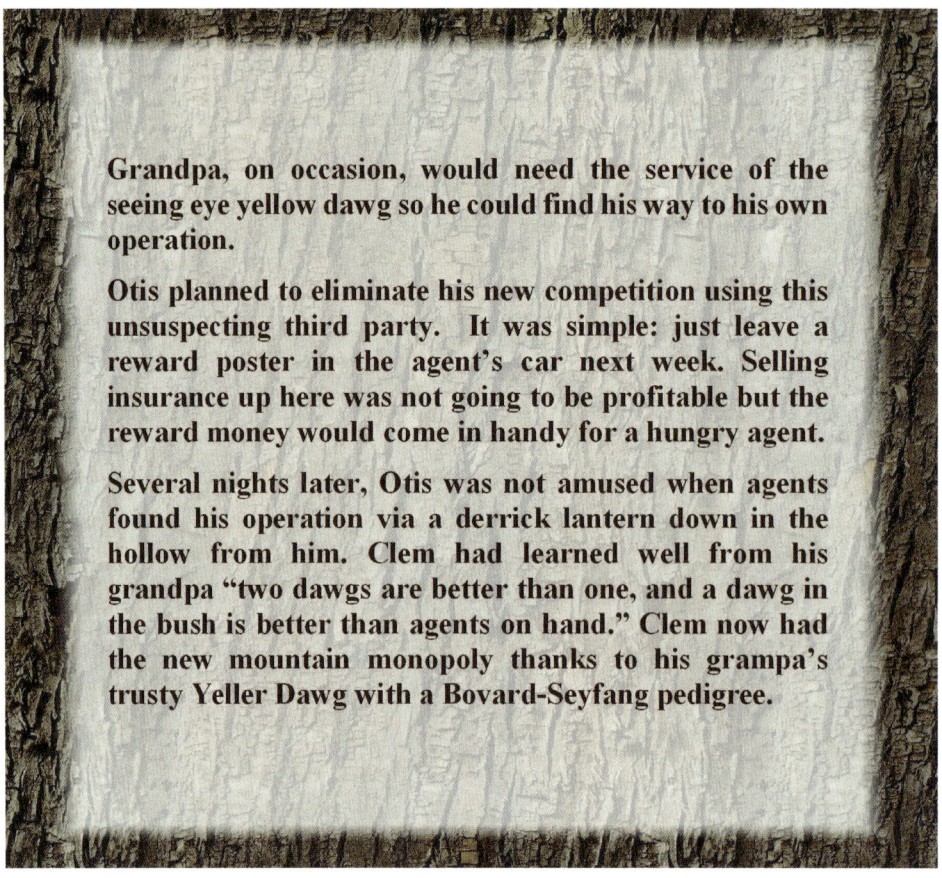

Grandpa, on occasion, would need the service of the seeing eye yellow dawg so he could find his way to his own operation.

Otis planned to eliminate his new competition using this unsuspecting third party. It was simple: just leave a reward poster in the agent's car next week. Selling insurance up here was not going to be profitable but the reward money would come in handy for a hungry agent.

Several nights later, Otis was not amused when agents found his operation via a derrick lantern down in the hollow from him. Clem had learned well from his grandpa "two dawgs are better than one, and a dawg in the bush is better than agents on hand." Clem now had the new mountain monopoly thanks to his grampa's trusty Yeller Dawg with a Bovard-Seyfang pedigree.

Note: Bovard-Seyfang made oil patch equipment.
Clems surviving Yeller Dawg courtesy of his widow.

Take a Walk in the Forest

The window of opportunity often appears to be flawed

Never short yourself on the tools of your trade: well salve, a hammer and rags keep the Bovard-Bradford engine running the pump jacks.

Bob Jordan

Ingrown "misery whip" (crosscut saw). Is this the place
where the logger ran out of gas before chainsaws were invented?

Yellow birch tries to trip the hard maple

Yellow birch ballet

Mutual support

(Left)
Trees are taking over the old
ski slope This held up
the rope tow in the 60s

(Below)
The mighty oak returns from
whence it came and so do we, to
discover more interesting curiosities.

Hope you enjoyed the walk.
Maybe we can take a hike again some day.

From the Author

I feel extremely fortunate that my career calling hit me at an early age. I was the kid in kindergarten with his nose pressed to the window watching whatever was happening outside. Leaves dropping or buds popping – it was and still is worth witnessing.

Kids usually get candy in their Easter basket. My parents gave me freeze-dried chili con carne. Easter vacation meant my folks wouldn't see me or my friend Pete for a week, as we would be camping and exploring. Later in years, they became suspicious when, after a week of camping, we would return with unused chili concarne and some spent shotgun shells. (When people would say, "Easter is going to be late this year" we knew why, it was because a few rabbits were missing).

The love of the outdoors took me to Wilderness Survival School in Montana (an extension of Easter vacation) US Forest Service in Mendocino CA, College of Forestry SUNY at Syracuse, Helicopter Logging in the Catskills & Adirondacks, and now forestry consulting with my son Jason in rural western NY & PA.

Trees, people, wildlife – it all can make for some interesting combinations. I have found through the years that if you cannot mix well with people, stay out of forestry. One has to evaluate people as well as the woodlot. There are intangible rewards in this profession like helping a family save the family farm from the taxman, or being able to pay down crippling debt, a young man's cancer co- pay, or seeing a father's joy as he proudly shows a picture of his son or daughter with their first deer.

Credits

I would like to give credit to my son Jason for his astute powers of observation and help making this endeavor possible. Jason, my daughter Kelly, and my wife Robin all deserve credit for sticking it out through thick 'n' thin.

To Steve Russo, Mike & Joanne Wellman, these people, whom I helped inspire, gave me the incentive to hopefully inspire others. After a walk with Mike & Joanne, she announced to Mike to skip the flowers for Mother's Day. She wanted a small chain saw! (The following year she wanted a bigger one.)

To my folks who were wise enough to teach me the value of the phrase "blessed are those who can laugh at themselves, for they shall never cease to be amused." I am still laughing at and amusing myself.

Made in the USA
Charleston, SC
09 December 2013